DATE DUE			

641.59   Duvall, Jill.   **160871**

DUV   Chef Ki is serving
c.1   dinner!

ALICE GUSTAFSON ELEMENTARY LRC

Career Ed., '99

Chef Ki Is Serving Dinner!

written by
JILL D. DUVALL

photographs by
LILI DUVALL

Reading Consultant
LINDA CORNWELL
Learning Resource Consultant
Indiana Department of Education

CHILDREN'S PRESS® A Division of Grolier Publishing
New York • London • Hong Kong • Sydney • Danbury, Connecticut

Special thanks to Duane Plank and his students at Glen Mills Schools, and Erika Romberg

Library of Congress Cataloging-in-Publication Data
Duvall, Jill.
    Chef Ki is serving dinner! / written by Jill D. Duvall ; photographs by Lili Duvall ; reading consultant, Linda Cornwell.
        p.   cm. — (Our neighborhood)
    Summary: Describes the work of a Korean American and his wife as they run their neighborhood restaurant in Virginia.
    ISBN 0-516-20313-4 (lib. bdg.)—ISBN 0-516-26148-7 (pbk.)
    1. Cookery, Korean—Juvenile literature. 2. Restaurants—Juvenile literature. 3. Cooks—Juvenile literature. [1. Cooks. 2. Restaurants. 3. Occupations.] I. Duvall, Lili, ill. II. Cornwell, Linda. III. Title. IV. Series: Our neighborhood.
    TX724.5.K65D88   1997
    641.59519—dc20
                                                                96-34902
                                                                    CIP
                                                                     AC

Photographs ©: Lili Duvall

Who cooks when we go out to eat?

In his restaurant, Chef Ki will make
dinner for us!

Chef Ki owns two restaurants in his neighborhood.

He creates dishes that taste delicious.

Chef Ki likes to cook chops.
He serves them with tasty,
fresh vegetables.

Sometimes, he chooses foods because of their colors.

His dishes look like works of art.

In the kitchen, Chef Ki gets his ingredients and utensils ready . . .

. . . to make one of his favorite recipes, clam chowder.

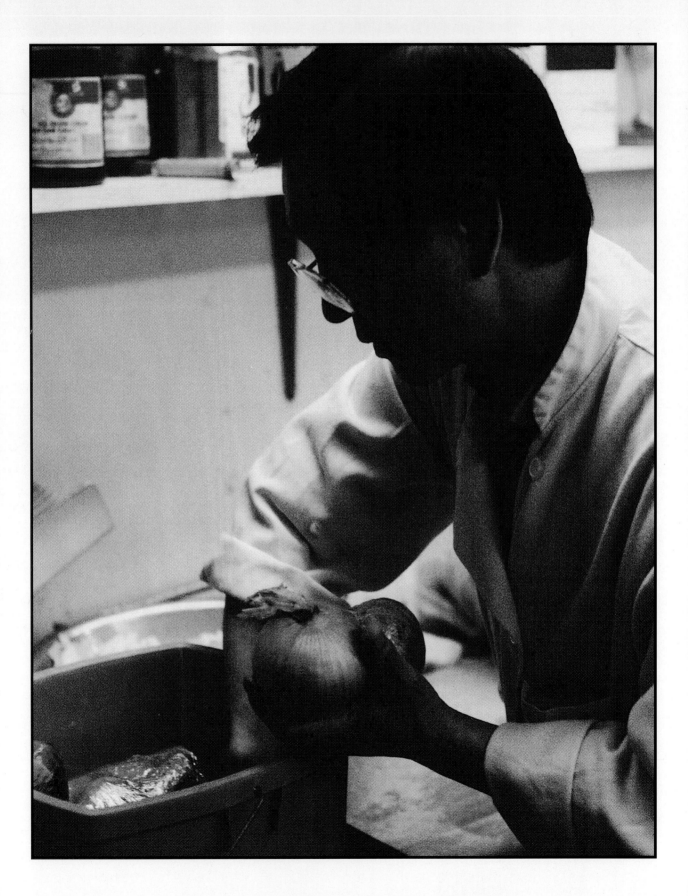

Cooking is fun,
but it takes lots of work.

Hard work doesn't bother Chef Ki.
He spends hours chopping onions,
cabbages, and other vegetables.

Customers are happy to have Chef Ki visit their tables. He wants to be sure they are enjoying their dinners.

Back in the kitchen, dessert is on the stove. Chef Ki's wife is on duty stirring the sugar.

The dessert looks beautiful when it is served to the customers.

Watching the chef cook is fun.
But eating is even better!

Sometimes, people want food for a party at home. They call Chef Ki.

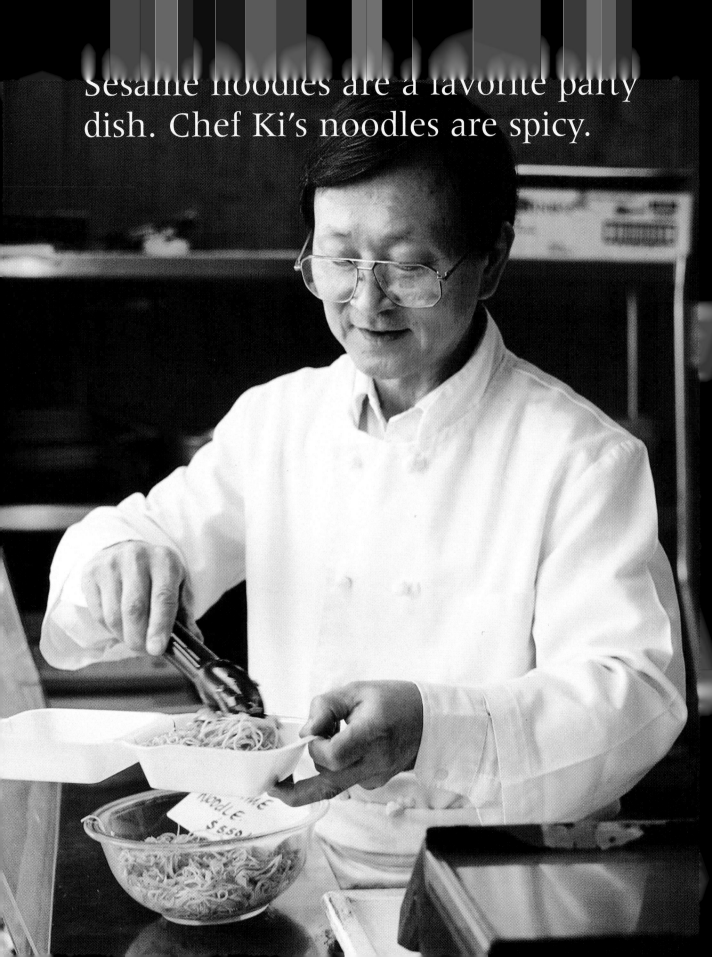

Sesame noodles are a favorite party dish. Chef Ki's noodles are spicy.

Chef Ki started to cook when he was a young man growing up in Korea. Other chefs taught him many things when he came to the United States. He keeps learning, even though he already knows how to cook all kinds of food.

Chef Ki believes that delicious, healthy food is important for his community.

Meet the Photographer and the Author

Lili Duvall decided when she was in her teens that she wanted to take pictures. She is now a professional photographer and taking pictures of children is her favorite work. Her home and studio are in Maryland.

Jill Duvall, Lili's writing partner, is also her mother. Jill likes living near Washington, D.C., because much of her studying and writing is about the government. Jill feels that writing is very important and even takes her writing to the beach!